A new way to enjoy Warcraft

Are you a Blood Elf Hunter? Or an Orc Mage? Do you love to Raid or Quest? Or are you a P.V.P. (Player verses Player) God? Or R.P. (Role Play) Master…? It really does not matter for this new way of enjoying the World of Warcraft is suited for all races, fractions and all sorts of game play adventure. I, Don "Broken Brain" Welbourne have started writing the R.P. adventures of my Toon into a book series taken from my characters diary who has been playing since the beginning.

Quest Tales

Starting with the first book "The Quest for Nimicie" Available on amazon and Kindle Dec. 2019 as well as "read by the author" weekly Readings and illustrations on our YouTube channel coming Dec. 2019

Back Cover:

The Moonshiner's Recipe Bible

Well I did it! I finally deciphered Grandpas old chicken scratches and Great Grandpas hieroglyphics and "done wrote me one hell of a fine Moonshine recipe book!" For all kinds of spirits Corn mash Whiskey, Gin, Vodka, Rum, Screech You name it! If it can be made in a Still or a bathtub I got the best recipe for it. Coming from a long, long line of moon shiners and though I'd never admit to doing it myself, It has been born and bred into me and is a subject I am an expert on. So if you want the best mash or need to learn how to build a Still without blowing yourself to pieces you need...

High Spirits... The Moonshiner's Recipe Bible.

My Grandpa: Donald Welbourne: "Don't shock your mash! Add your dry goods first start with the sugar then your corn meal then use your fist to make a little volcano in the mixture and poor your yeast in the volcano keep'n the sugar and yeast separate. Let that sit for about twenty minutes to half an hour to let the yeast come to room temperature before you add your wet ingredients."

KILL ME QUICK SHINE

10 gallons of water 5 Lbs of sugar

3 Lbs of cracked corn 3 Lbs of rye

1 Lb of raisins 1 keg of yeast

Mix ingredients together and ferment for 7 to 10 days or until the yeast quits working. Strain and distill.

The Late Great Grandpa Welbourne: "My father taught me to keep yeast in brown paper, fold it good and dip it in bees wax then keep it in a cool spot." "It keeps your yeast fresh I don't know how exactly but I've always done it that way." But I guessing this was way before refrigerators and vacuumed sealed jars.

WELCHES FROZEN GRAPE JUICE MOONSHINE BRANDY

10 cans (11.5 oz) Welches 100% frozen grape concentrate 7 Lbs granulated sugar

water to make 5 gallons wine or distillers yeast

Bring 5 quarts of water to boil and dissolve the sugar in the water. Remove from heat and add frozen concentrate. Add additional water to make five gallons and pour into secondary. Add remaining ingredients except yeast. Cover with cloth fastened with rubber band and set aside 12 hours. after cooling to proper yeast temperature, add activated yeast and recover with cloth. Ferment 30 days..

Moonshine wisdom:

Whiskey made from corn exposed to horse shit will have a flavor disagreeable to most.

Introduction

First I like to say that all the stories and recipes in here are written exactly as they were Read or told. That being said my friends and family and people I've interviewed do span Canada and even some Americans. So you will encounter Nefenease, FrEnglish , Torontonian, Manitobian, Saskenease, Albertian BCish and even American "Y'all". I just want it known I'm not an idiot and DO know how to use spell check!

Thank You

About when I was twelve or so my Grandfather passed away and I went with my dad to clean out his place and I remember dad throwing out this brown leather satchel that grandpa always tried to hide. Well I rescued it from the trash without dad knowing and stored it away. For years I couldn't read the writing in it all on old, browned scraps of paper I romanticized they were letters from WWII but as I got older and use to reading other peoples hand writing I finally figured it out, to my shock , that it was the family recipe book, and not one apple pie in the lot.

. Names have been changed for protection.

THANK YOU

To all the relatives and friends who have contributed to this book I'm sure Grandpa would be rolling over in his grave to know his recipes went public.

Table of Contents

The Book of "Wisdom"

Chapter 1

How to build a still

"Old Jethro's next door's a-makin' moonshine again," the wife told her husband. "How can you tell?" he asked. "Did you smell it?"

"Nope. But a bunch of mice from over to his place came over here this morning and beat the crap out of our cats."

If you're reading this, I assume you are interested in the theoretical transformation of a relatively weak alcoholic mixture into a relatively strong alcoholic mixture. That is, the distillation of whisky.

If you don't know about the early stages of whisky distillation, here is a quick round-up:

Take some grain, and allow it to sprout. Just as it starts to sprout, quickly kill it by drying. It is now a "malted grain". Mix the malted grain with hot water and stir until you get bored - you are dissolving the sugars from the grain into the water. Filter out the solids, and add yeast. Keep the mixture slightly warm (and sealed from the air) until the yeast has turned the sugar into alcohol. You now have a wash that is ready to be distilled.

Apparently, the wash has a strength and taste similar to beer, so maybe you would like to start there.

Distillation is the process of separating a mixture of liquids with different boiling points. In this case, we're trying to separate ethanol (alcohol) from water. Pure ethanol boils at 78.4oC, and pure water boils at 100oC, so heating the wash will make the ethanol boil off first.

Step 1What you need

A still has three separate parts - something to heat the liquid, something to help water vapours condense before they escape the apparatus and something to cool and trap the alcoholic vapours.

I will refer to these parts as the vat, column and condenser. You also need a thermometer with a scale that goes to at least +100oC.

Since this is more a guide to function than form, you may choose to use different materials to those suggested, such as paying out for all-copper fittings. This is by no means an exhaustive tutorial, so if you are planning to produce quality drinking-spirits on a regular basis (as opposed to something merely flammable), you may even want to invest in a purpose-built still. Just remember (again) that, in the majority of countries where you can read this Instruct able, you need to check the legality of distilling alcoholic beverages for personal use

THE PROCESS OF A SIMPLE HOMEMADE STILL

A simple still can be made from a test tube, some heavy rubber hose, and an ordinary bottle. When making moonshine, you will need a far bigger contraption, but the purpose of putting this here is so that you can see the process. This still is for distilling water.

Secure a stopper for the test tube, and bore a hole through the center of the stopper, into which fits a small piece of tube. The bottle is also fitted with a stopper containing a piece of tube, and both bottle and test tube are connected with the rubber tube.

The test tube is partly filled with water and supported or held over an alcohol lamp. The bottle should stand in a basin of cold water. When the water in the test tube begins to boil the steam passes over to the bottle, where it condenses. The basin should be supplied with cold water as soon as it begins to get warm. The rubber tube will not stand the heat very long and if the still is to be used several times, a metal tube should be supplied to connect the test tube and bottle

THE BASICS OF MAKING MOONSHINE AND WHAT YOU NEED TO KNOW

Ingredients Corn meal Sugar Water Yeast

Malt extract

Now you also need the following for you to be able to know how to make moonshine: A Mash Tub, or Fermenter

A Still

A Condenser

Now, not everyone has copper stills lying around in their own backyards. However, most kitchens have a pressure cooker, a kitchen sink and a stove. And of course you will need a 20 gallon drum. However, a new, metal garbage bin will do the trick, if you can't find anything else. With a few other minor adoptions, you have yourself a home made moonshine still.

Method

Fill your 20 gallon container with 10 gallons of water. Make sure that it is at 120 degrees Fahrenheit.

You now need to scald the meal by adding it to the water, a little at time, followed by the sugar. Stir well.

You will now need to set the drum or garbage can on a very slow fire. Make sure that you do not scorch your mash and the temperature must be kept below 145 degrees F. else the heat will prevent the starch from being converted into sugar. Leave for about half an hour.

When your mash is a very thin gruel like consistency, take it off the heat and cook it down by cooling the outside of the container with water. You can do this by placing the

container in the sink or the like, and filling up the sink with water to bring the temperature down.

When your mash is cool enough to stir your finger through it without being burned, we need to check that there has been enough conversion from starch to sugar. To do this we need to do the iodine test.

Take a small amount of mash and place a drop of iodine on the top of it. If it turns a dark purple we know that there are still starches present that haven't been totally converted into sugar. If this is the result, put the mash back on a low heat for another half an hour. If there is only a light purple, then we can continue to the next stage of learning how to make moonshine.

We now add about a pint of malt extract and a cake of yeast that has been well crumbled and mixed in a little cup of warm water to dissolve first.

You may find that your mash is very thick at this stage. It is fine to add some warm water to the mash to thin it out. Don't add hot water as this will kill of the yeast.

Place your drum of mash in a warm place - about 65 degrees and leave it for 3 days. At this stage you may cover it with a cloth if you have a danger of rats or insects falling into your mash. However, if you don't have these dangers, leaving it open will encourage wild yeast to enter your mash, giving it a distinct flavor.

You will see your mash rising in the drum with a foamy head to it. This is normal. When the froth stops growing, your mash is ready. Too much acid in your mash while it is fermenting will result in vinegar. Therefore, you will need to check your mash with litmus paper or if you have it diabetic test strips to see if your mash is still safe. If you find that the litmus paper turns blue on contact with your mash, or only a slight tinge of pink, it is fine.

So, in the next process of learning how to make moonshine you will want to build your still, while your mash is fermenting. Take the old pressure cooker and drill a 1/4 inch hole into the lid of the pressure cooker / pressure canner. Now take your copper tubing and get it through the hole, making sure that it is projecting no more than an inch into your pot. The tubing should fit in very tight, without the possibility of it coming out under pressure from the gases.

Now we need to run the copper tubing from the pressure cooker on the stove to the sink. At least 3 feet of the copper piping should be left in the sink.

To condense the vapor into moonshine, we now need to convert a thermos jug for this purpose. Take a 1 gallon thermos jug with a tap / faucet and remove the tap. Now take the excess copper wire beyond the three feet that is sitting in the sink and coil it by wrapping it around an object multiple times so that it will fit snuggly into the jug. Have an extension of copper wire coming out from where the faucet used to be.

During the distilling process the thermos jug will be placed under an open cold tap where the jug will always be filled with cold water, and excess water will flow through the space where the faucet used to be, flowing over the copper extension through this gap.

In learning how to make moonshine you will soon notice that after 3 or 4 days the foam on the mash has stopped frothing and being active and you are left with a light golden- brown liquid called still-beer. We will use this to fill up our pressure cooker.

Fill the pressure cooker up to only 4/5ths of its capacity, but make sure that you strain it first using either a clean, open- weave tea towel or some cheesecloth.

Place the lid on the pressure cooker and heat up the still-beer over a very low heat. Make sure, that at this point you have the water running through your thermos jug and you have a receptacle below the end of the copper tubing to catch the alcohol vapor.

Allow at least 1/2 cup of moonshine to accumulate in the cup and then throw it away down the drain. This is a vital step when learning how to make moonshine. NEVER drink this first distill. It is not just paint stripper to your insides, but his highly toxic to your system and you are putting your life in danger by drinking this liquid. People have lost their sight, damaged their organs and worse, even died, from drinking this first distill.

After each lot of still-beer in the pressure cooker has been distilled you will be left with about a gallon and a half to two gallons of alcohol known as 'low wines'.

What you need to do now, is to re-distill this liquid as it contains too much water. The pressure cooker needs to be rinsed out and dried before we add our low wines back in to the pressure cooker.

Again, place over a very low heat and wait for the vapor to emerge. Again we have to throw the first lot of vapor away. About 1/2 cup again. When the first appearance of a white liquid emerges then we know that we are the path to having made our first batch of hopefully, drinkable moonshine!!!

However, before we get too excited, what we have made is probably rocket fuel, as it is about 140% proof. What we need to do is to find a hygrometer, and mix enough water with the whiskey to get it down to a more drinkable 100% proof. If you don't have a hygrometer, do it the old fashioned way. Take a quart jar and fill it half with moonshine. Now shake it gently and sit it on a flat surface. If there are bubbles half above and half below the liquid, then you have the right proof.

A final word about learning how to make moonshine, don't be tempted to use plastic tubing to replace the copper tubing as the heat and activities of the distillation process will cause chemicals from the plastic to be leached into your moonshine. Lastly, use your common sense when making this stuff, and adopt safety procedures at all times, knowing that what you are working with is a volatile substance, that needs attention and concentration at all times.

How to Make Moonshine in 21 Easy Steps

Using a Pressure Cooker Still and a Recipe How to make moonshine at home using a pressure cooker still with our moonshine instructions, and we'll give you a peach moonshine recipe. However, please check with your local authorities to see if it is legal to make moonshine in your area. Some countries do not allow it at all, while some do, but only for personal consumption.

However, despite the blanket ban in some countries in making moonshine whiskey, many people still make moonshine when homesteading today, and many more are looking for instructions on how to make moonshine at home. So, for the good old economic adage of 'supply and demand' we will oblige, and show you how to make moonshine.

However, please be careful when you are making moonshine whiskey, and know the dangers. If you don't control the temperature properly you could end up poisoning yourself, and the same goes when you have not gotten rid of contaminates during the distillation process, or drinking the first distill. You also need to realize that your homemade still has the potential to explode from a build up of gases if you have added your fruit or corn too early.

Finally, you should only use moonshine stills made from copper as many people are unaware that they can get lead poisoning from using contaminated metal containers for their distillation equipment. So, you see, there is a lot to learn on how to make moonshine.

Moonshine, is a term used to describe making distilled alcohol at home, especially in places where it would be illegal to do so. Where I come from, we call it "mampoer" or "witblits" (white lightning), and it is traditionally made with peaches, so basically a peach moonshine. However, you can make distilled alcohol out of many fruits and vegetables, and we will try and explain the process as easily as possible and soon you will know how to make moonshine.

A day in the woods

While watching a friend I noticed he does not use a hydrometer but he reads the bead. Here is how he does it. He takes a quart mason jar half full of the distillate with a lid on it. He holds the top of the jar in his right hand and hits the inside of his left hand with the bottom of the jar three times. This causes the distillate to bubble inside the jar and before the bubbles settle he turns the jar onto its side and it will break into three consistent pools. Thus he said is 103 proof. He was right because I checked it with a hydrometer and its between 100 and 104 every time. Nothing replaces experience

The still ...He has had several different sizes over the past several years but all of them were made of copper. Typically they were pot stills that had thumpers attached to them. He primed the thumpers with what he refers to as backings. Which I have interpreted as (what was at the end of the previous run.) The actual boiler was surrounded with a type of clay and rock mixture and was heated with propane burners. The boiler did not sit on top of the heat source. It was heated indirectly. The large still that he used for corn whiskey had a tank that set beside the still with tubing that ran from the cap of the still through the container. This was filled with mash and was preheated by the current alcohol of the

mash being distilled. When he had gotten to the end of the first run the old mash was discarded through a valve at the bottom of the still and the new preheated mash was drained into the still from a valve at the top therefore eliminating the slow heat up of the new mash. Just in a few minutes there would be distillate running. The cooling was done by a 1inch worm in a 55 gallon barrel with cold water being piped up from the creek.

....

Moonshine Wisdom:

{A Collection of tips and tricks}

Moonshine wisdom:

"Whiskey made from corn exposed to horse shit will have a flavor disagreeable to most".

....

"Siphon off the liquor, leaving behind any dead snakes, rats, birds or other varmints. Put it in the still. Fire it off slowly."

....

If you want to make your own recipe, keep in mind grain contains about 60% fermentable material. About 1 to 1.5 kg of grain is normally used / 4 L (1 US gal) as the mash is quite thick, the rest can be sugar. 1 kg grain/4 L water would be equivalent to 600 g sugar/4 L, so you could add an additional 200 g sugar/4 L to give a 10% alcohol yield which beer yeasts should handle. The crushed grain needs 10% crushed malted grain for malting. e.g. a generic moonshine mash for 20 l could be 5 kg crushed grain, 500 g crushed malted grain, and 1 kg sugar. Other combinations are possible.

.... A good rule of thumb is that there is one US gallon of 100 proof whiskey in a bushel of corn. Also, one gallon in 25 pounds of sugar

.... The Late Great Grandpa Welbourne: "My father taught me to keep yeast in brown paper, fold it good and dip it in bees wax then keep it in a cool spot." "It keeps your yeast fresh I don't know how exactly but I've always done it that way." But I guessing this was way before refrigerators and vacuumed sealed jars.

....

Cousin Mark

Nearly 40 years ago, I took a sample of grandpaw's whiskey and several storebought whiskeys to the lab & ran 'em through the gas cromatagraph. Grampa's was much more pure !!

Mark found an old recipe ...

"It is many years ago that this Norwegian recipe was used and I put it down here just for a matter of record. It would be a blessing if modern distillers would adopt this old pure old formula.

Take one bushel of corn meal and one-fourth bushel of malted barley meal. Place them in a large kettle and cover with enough good well water to cover the meal at least four or five inches. Slowly bring to a low boil and simmer for at least one hour, preferably two

hours, and keep adding water to keep up the water level as the meal absorbs the water. Stir to keep from burning. This cooking or mashing gives the malted barley enzymes a chance to change the starch in the corn to maltose which is an easily fermented sugar. Yeast cannot change cornstarch or any other starch to sugar. Remove the pot from the heat. Let cool and strain the liquid from the cooked meal into a fifty gallon oak barrel. Add well water to the cooked meal mass. This is called "sparging" it and stir and again squeeze out the liquid. Repeat until all of the liquids possible are washed out of the cooked meal. Add about one hundred pounds of corn sugar or invert sugar or cane sugar, if you do not have the others, and stir in well. Fill the barrel about three- fourths full by adding good well water. Take a saccharometer and test the solution. By adding sugar or water, adjust the solution so that it will produce sixteen percent alcohol. Add a gallon of top fermenting yeast "starter" or about five pounds of yeast skimmed off from a previous mash or bakers' yeast if you have no top fermenting yeast. Put a cover on the barrel as yeast produces alcohol much faster if it does not have too much of a supply of air. Never set a mash where it is windy or drafty as then the yeast will turn the sugar into carbon dioxide and water, not carbon dioxide and alcohol. Let ferment at not colder than 75 degrees. Test the wort or liquid every day with a saccharometer. Let the saccharometer go between 996 and 998.

Then siphon and run the wort through a pot still, not a patent still, in not less than three hours time producing not more than ten to twelve gallons of whiskey running about 90 proof. Strain the whiskey through a three-foot-thick layer of hard maple charcoal. Add one quart of dry sherry wine and the juice from a level tablespoon of nutmeg boiled in a half cup of water to the whiskey. Store in oak barrels or in glass jugs with a few oak chips in the bottom. The oak barrels or the oak chips will give the whiskey color. No modern maker has ever equalled this whiskey and will admit it if asked. It is so smooth that you can drink it down like water, needs no mixing with anything. Any Scandinavian worth of the name was highly insulted if you ever tried to diulte this drink of the gods." Bull Cook and Authentic Historical Recipes -- G.L. Herter, circa 1969

Only use grains if you are after flavour (eg making a bourbon or whisky), or if for some reason they are really cheap for you to obtain. Generally, a reflux still will strip out all the flavours and leave a neutral spirit. But, you can actually use a reflux still to make flavoured spirits such as whisky, provided you detune them a little, and then carefully pay attention to how you make the cut.

.... An excellent way to remove the grains after fermentation is to have used a "grain bag" - eg a large bag made of mesh or muslin to hold the grains. You then simply lift this out of

the mash when they're all spent, and its easy to rinse them. Far easier than using strainers, seives etc.

.... Big tip ! It generally pays not to distill a grain wort with a still with an internal element. You get too many solids / complex sugars remaining that WILL burn onto the element. The whisky will stink, and the burnt flavour can't be removed. And its bloody difficult to clean the element properly & remove all the char (trust me). The one thing all the old time moonshiners always talk about is the skill needed to "fire a still without scorchin' the whiskey". Jack has a theory "everyone should have 2 stills: one column equipped, run on heating elements (for sugar spirit), and one stovetop potstill (for whiskey and rum mashes)".

.... Don't empty the spent grains outa the fermenting pot just yet. You can use it to make seconds or " backins" as the old timers called it. To make 'good stuff' add another bushel of sprouted corn (no more yeast) . Let it work and repeat the above procedure.

To make rot gut for your brother-in-law add 20 pounds of sugar and proceed as above Keep in mind: Never, ever under any circumstances whatsoever let anything touch your whiskey except wood, stainless steel, copper or glass. Age your whiskey in charred oak barrels for at least a year. Or for small amounts, tale a wide mouth gallon jug. Add lump hardwood charcoal (NEVER use briquettes, only REAL charcoal). Fill with whiskey.

Age at least a year. Filter through a coffee filter & drink it.

.... END OF WISDOM............................

The Book of: "Shine"

Chapter 1 Shine on harvest moon

A man was walking down the street in a small Tennessee mountain town, when he sees another man walking toward him carrying a jug of moonshine and a shotgun.

Since this made him a little wary he decided to cross the street. To his dismay, the shotgun toting man crossed the street also. He then crossed again, but the other man crossed also.

Finally the shotgun toting man walked up to him, extending the jug and said "Here take a swig."

He then replied "No Thanks".

Then the other man raised the shotgun and pointed it right at him. "TAKE A SWIG !"

He then said "alright, alright...take it easy!"

He then took a big swig, almost coughing it up and gagged: "Holy   thats some nasty stuff!".

Then the man handed him the shotgun and said "Here, now you hold the shotgun on me while I take a swig"

Uncle Talbert Reckons ...

I've always gone with my tried and true, except for brandies and split-brandies. LOVE

making split-brandies!! Large batches of mash ferment the best! Like in 55 gal wooden or plastic (new of course) barrels.

My notes on sloppin back, ya'll folks've caLLed it yeast recyclin. That's just fine (must be city folk) Ya'll alright. I luv ya jess 'th same.

Ok, see... What I'm tryin to say hear see, is   After yor first run 'O mash, save about half

'O that slop thar in thet cooker 'O yors and put thet rite back in thet there barrel. OK, bucket for you short runnrs. Add half agin as much new fresh grain to hit. DON'T put n'more yeast inner.

She's got enuff rite thar whare shes at. OK, put the usual
amounts of sugar rite in thar as well. Watchr work up a STORM
and make sum goooood likker my frens. Specially on the thrice
batch like I toldja b'fore. Now do this up to 6-7 times. Toldja
thet one too. Man, ya'll gonna make sum goood sh*t, I tell ya.

Peach Moonshine Recipe

Shine

Take a large barrel, or two, of very ripe yellow peaches and
mash them up in large drums. There is no need to clean them.
Now leave them for about 2 weeks to rot and ferment.

During this time the fruit will give off a lot of gas, so there is no
point in putting any lids on here at this stage, however, you
should have a cover or some sort that will still allow the gases to
escape and keep the insects out.

When the bubbles subside, the mash is ready to distill. Don't
leave the mash too long or it will go sour and you'll end up with
peach vinegar.

Heat the mash in the still, which is a big copper kettle, and heat
the fermented peaches to just below boiling, so that the alcohol
comes off.

The alcohol boils off before the water and is trapped by a condensation pipe. The condensate is collected in a bucket and, for really top quality peach moonshine, it may be re-distilled.

....

The Fine Art of Moonshining

Fermenter - barrel (55 gals or 220 l) 1/2 bushel (30 lb or 14 kg) Corn Meal a)

3 & 1/2 lbs (1.5 kg) malted corn

2 handfuls raw rye to form cap on fermenting mash

Optional - sugar, 40 lbs (20 kg) in 2 lots - 10 lb (5 kg) then 30 lb (15 kg) Yeast not mentioned.

b)

1 bushel (60 kg) corn meal

1 & 1/2 gal (6 l) malted corn Yield -

Pure Corn 1.5 gal (4-6 l)/bushel (28 lb or 13 kg)

Corn & Sugar 6 gal (24 l)/bushel (28 lb or 13 kg)

Shawn is learning corn whisky from an elder neighbour...

He has learned this through trial and error but he is willing to try and teach me. For example there is not allot of exact science that he uses. Its mostly by site, smell, tasting and touching.

....

Quick Moonshine

5 kg (10 lb) crushed grain (grits) 2 and 1/2 kg (5 lb) sugar

20 L (5 US gals) water

2 tbsp acid (2 g acid/litre)- a pH 4-5 is required.

2 tsp amylase enzymes (alpha-, beta-, gluco-) or 750 g (1 and 1/2 lb) crushed malted barley grain (15% by weight)

Suitable ale yeast Yeast nutrient (D.A.P.)

This should produce about 10-12%abv.

No pre-soaking of the crushed grain is required as there is sufficient sugars for the yeast to begin the fermentation process while the grain soaks.

....

Moonshine

A "genuine" moonshine recipe, as still being used by Deb Brewer is ...

5 gallon bucket all grain horse feed (we use MannaPro Hi Grain sweet feed)

one package of yeast (using bread yeast now--others will increase quality and ferment time)

5 pounds sugar water

Put enough feed to cover bottom of 5 gallon bucket a good 4 inches deep Add 5 pounds of sugar. Fill 1/2 full with warm water--warm enough to melt sugar but not so hot as to kill yeast. Mix until sugar is dissolved. Add yeast and mix some more finish filling with warm water--again not so hot to kill the yeast. Cover with lid--our lid has a little cap that screws on, leave it loose to breathe.

4-5 days later it's ready to run! This is an old-timer recipe and works quite well. Our liquor is always 170-190 proof. You can substitute corn meal for the grain (horse feed) but I don't recommend this for pot stills cuz you can't filter it well enough. The meal will settle and burn in the bottom of your still. The old-fashion way of making corn liquor-- with real corn--just is not feasible time wise.

....

MOUNTAIN DEW RECIPE

In making "Mountain Dew" or "White Lightning'" the first step is to convert the starch of the grain into sugar. (Commercial distillers use malt.) This is done by "sprouting" the corn. Shelled, whole corn is covered with warm water in a container with a hole in the bottom. Place a hot cloth over it. Add warm water from time to time as it drains. Keep in a warm place for about 3 days or until corn has 2 inch sprouts. Dry it and grind it into meal. Make mush (or mash) with boiling water. Add rye mash that has been made the same way, if you have it. Yeast (1/2 pound per 50 gallons of mash) may be added to speed up the fermentation if you have it. Without it, 10 or more days will be required instead of about 4. In either case, it must be kept warm. When the mash gets through "working" or bubbling up and settles down, it is then ready to run. At this stage, the mash has been converted into carbonic acid and alcohol. It is called "wash" or beer and it is sour..

....

Stonewalls Honey Shine

One quart of honey per 1 1/2 gallons of water. One 4 oz Package of Turbo yeast per 10

gallons of mash. Ferments for 7 to 14 days and then distill.

....

SWEET FEED MOONSHINE # 5 gallon bucket of sweet feed

(Sweet feed has several different grains and molasses making it a great tasting whiskey.) one package of yeast (using distillers yeast will increase quality and quantity) # 5 pounds sugar # water Put enough feed to cover bottom of 5 gallon bucket a good 4 inches deep Add 5 pounds of sugar. Fill 1/2 full with boiling water. Mix until sugar is dissolved. Let it set for 90 minutes and then finish filling with cool water. Add the yeast after it has cooled to the recommended temperature on the yeast label. Cover with lid--our lid has a little cap that screws on, leave it loose to breathe. 4-5 days later it's ready to run! This is an old-timer recipe and works quite well. My liquor is always 150-180 proof. I don't recommend this for pot stills unless you filter it by pouring it through a pillow case into a 5 gallon bucket after it has finished fermenting. Otherwise the meal will settle and burn in the bottom of your still. Some folks leave the solids in the pillow case and tie it off where it will not touch the bottom of the still.

....

TANGLE-FOOT MOONSHINE

Fermenter - barrel (55 gals) Option 1

1/2 bushel (30 lb) Corn Meal 3 & 1/2 lbs malted corn

2 handfuls raw rye to form cap on fermenting mash Optional - sugar, 40 lbs in 2 lots - 10 lb then 30 lb 1 cup of Yeast.

Option 2

1 bushel corn meal

1 & 1/2 gal malted corn Yield -

Pure Corn 1.5 gal/bushel (28 lb) Corn & Sugar 6 gal/bushel (28 lb) 1 cup of yeast

....

School Teachers Shine:

Wheat Bran ~~~~> a five gal. bucketfull and then another half bucket.

Sugar ~~~~~~~~~~> 50 lbs. (Sam's club is the deal!) Fleishman's (Bakers)Yeast ~~~~> 3 packs

Filler up with water.

That'll make anywhere from 6-8 gallons of fine liquor, uuhhh Fuel, yeah fuel...

First batch in will ferment 5-7 days and then form a cap. If you "slop-back" that mash it will work off in 3 days after the yeast is growing up to around 6-7 times. Then it's time to start a fresh mash. When the cap falls, and the beers getting a bitter taste to it, she's ready to run. If it has any sweet taste at all it is too "green" and will not produce as much and will kick and buck and act wild in the still with a posibility of blowing the cap. Not a happy experience. It can ruin yor hole day. Never knew I could run so damn fast... I know a few good common sense tricks on what to do when as far as the mash goes. If is it not workin good or too good for that matter. You make all the alcohol in the barrel. If you don't do it right there, the prettiest still in the world won't do you any good at all. Still just separates the juice from the water. Hell, you all know all that by now, I'm sure of that.

Wheat bran: when U go to the feed store where they mill 'th grain, specify unsalted wheat bran. If the feller looks at you twice or reaaal hard, mumble kinda under yor breath, "damn horse is so constipated..."

Sugar: Go 't Sam's Club or anywhere thet they would sell you sum 50 pound saks 'O sugar and load a couple up on yor cart. Take 'em to 'th check out counter. Whistle a tune, soft and slow like. Don't forget to whistle... And if the checkout countr gurl looks at you funny like or says sumthin smart, you jess say, "Yep, the church is havin a bake sale t'morrow and they all put me in charge of buyin 'th sugars." This'll covr you fer buyin all them packs of Fleishman's Bakers yeast too.

Werks for me...

....

Kentucky Sweet Mash

20 L water (5 gal)

2 kg (4 and 1/2 lb) corn meal 500 g (1 lb)

50 g malted grain

....

'Alcohol Fuel Manual' grain mash

20 L water (5 gal)

4 kg (9 lb) crushed grain

400 g (1 lb) crushed malted grain NOT FOR DRINKING

....

Moonshine : 'Old John Barley'

20 L water (5 gal)

2 kg (4 and 1/2 lb) crushed corn 700 g (1 and 1/2 lb) crushed barley 300 g (3/4 lb) malt syrup

1 kg (2 and 1/2 lb) molasses

....

Moonshine

20 L water (5 gal)

3 kg (7 lb)crushed grain

4.5 kg (10 lb) sugar

....

Moonshine

20 L water (5 gal)

2 kg (4 and 1/2 lb) corn meal 300 g (1 lb) malted corn

2.5 kg (5 and 1/2) lb sugar

....

Moonshine

20 L water (5 gal)

6 kg corn meal (uncooked)

0.6 L malted corn

....

SWEET MASH MOON SHINE

1/2 bushel of corn meal in 55 gallon barrel 5 pounds of sugar

1/2 pounds of "Red Star" yeast

Scald the mixture with 5_10 gallons of boiling water fill barrel with water till five or six inches from the top.

cover barrel with cloth and wait till it quits working (about 2-3 days) cook mixture until it boils

put a hose with a stopper in the end and push it to the bottom. Blow out the stopper and siphon off the mixture until about 4 inches is left in the barrel

strain remaining liquid, put in cooker, cook it till it boils, then simmer. yields 4 gallons of 90 proof moon shine!!!

....

Quick Moonshine

5 kg (10 lb) crushed grain (grits) 2 and 1/2 kg (5 lb) sugar

20 L (5 US gals) water

2 tbsp acid (2 g acid/litre)- a pH 4-5 is required.

2 tsp amylase enzymes (alpha-, beta-, gluco-) or 750 g (1 and 1/2 lb) crushed malted barley grain (15% by weight)

Suitable ale yeast Yeast nutrient (D.A.P.)

This should produce about 10-12%abv.

No pre-soaking of the crushed grain is required as there is sufficient sugars for the yeast to begin the fermentation process while the grain soaks

....

SOUR MASH MOON SHINE

1 bushel of hard (seed) white corn bury corn in horse manure

pour 5 gallon of water over the corn corn sprouts in about two days remove corn and wash

roll the corn to crack it

put corn in a 55 gallon barrel add 1/2 bushel of corn meal add 5 pound of sugar

fill barrel with water

in 21 days a red skim will form and it is time to cook it put a hose with a stopper in the end and push it to the bottom. Blow out the stopper and siphon off the mixture until about 4 inches is left in the barrel

strain remaining liquid, put in cooker, cook it till it boils, then simmer. yields 1.5 gallons of 105 proof moon shine!!!

.... END OF SHINE..................................

The Book of: "Whiskey"

IF

The moonshine still you built on Endor is hidden so well even the Ewoks can't find it You might be a jedi Redneck

Your moonshine is made on a real moon.

You might be a jedi Redneck

History of Whiskey

For an extremely over-simplifed botany lesson: Plants exist to survive and reproduce.

They are only tasty to us by coincidence. A kernal of grain needs to be mostly a sugar form in order to grow larger than a sprout. The kernal is meant to supply the necessary food so that it can grow. But sugar is prone to spoilage and to rapid fermentation from natural yeasts and from insects. So the food is stored as starch for safekeeping. When needed, the kernal produces enzymes to convert that starch to sugar. You add malted grain to mashed grains to convert the starches in the entire bunch to sugar. Mashing is the process of heating grain to the point where the starches are released from the solid kernal.

The reason to ferment grain is to get the flavor from the grains and save it in your beverage. The cut off points when distilling determine how much flavor or odor is included in your beverage. Same theory as getting too much instant coffee in the cup. Too much makes it a nasty sip. Just enough makes it pleasant. Not enough makes it weak and watery.

You need to use grains to make a traditional whisky recipe. Otherwise you are making a clear vodka and then adding syrups to flavor it enough to call it whisky. If you grind up a steak and drop it on a bun after frying it, is it still called steak or is it hamburger? If a tree falls in the woods with no one around does it still make noise? If a man speaks when no women are around is he still wrong? Lots of questions with out clear answers.

The payoff for the effort that is invloved is the satisfaction knowing that you accomplished something diffucult, and did it with a certain amount of skill. Bragging rights are important sometimes. The proof is in the cup.

Where do you find cracked corn and other grains suitable for brewing with ? Try rural feed supliers. As long as you get the grain after the cracking process and before they add the fortifications to the animal feed you will be alright. Tell then you want cracked corn to make homemade corn meal or flour and they should give you the right stuff.

....

Scotch whisky

It is now generally agreed that there are six regions and these are based on taste as well as geographical location. Lowlands, Highlands, Speyside, Campbeltown, Islay, Islands. The distillate is 75%abv, which is diluted to 63.4%abv and stored in oak casks (average is a 250litre hogshead). Depending on casks used, the spirit picks up color and flavor. Casks that held bourbon, sherry and port are reused.

....

Irish whiskey

Irish whiskey differs from Scotch Whisky in that it is usually distilled 3 times. The malting process is also different as the Irish use sprouted barley dried in a closed kiln which is then mixed with unmalted barley before being ground into a grist. This can be said to account for the lightness of Irish whiskey and its 'non peaty' taste compared to Scotch.

....

American whiskey

North American whiskies are all-grain spirits that have been produced from a mash that usually mixes together corn, rye, wheat, barley and other grains in different proportions, the resulting distillate then generally aged in wooden barrels. These barrels may be new or used, and charred or uncharred on the inside, depending on the type of whiskey being made. The U.S. government requires that all whiskies have to be made from a grain mash and be distilled at 90%abv or less. The whisky has to be reduced to no more than 62.5%abv before being aged in new oak barrels (American white oak) and then be bottled at no more than 40%abv.

Why go to the bother of using grains ? and why do you need the malt present ? Cornfed explains ...

Malted grains: Are grains that are sprouted and then have the growth stopped. This process naturally produces the enzymes necessary to convert starch to sugars. The enzymes are called amylases. You can also get enzymes from a supplier and add them.

....

JD's Black Label Recipe

It consists of 80% corn, 12% rye, 8% malt (a high enzyme 6-row variety will be needed). Steep your ingredients in 140 to 150 degree water for about 1 to 1 1/2 hours. Wait until it has cooled to 68 degrees before adding your yeast. After fermentation, it is distilled once in a pot still with a thumper, then filtered through a 10 foot layer of maple charcoal (this takes about 4 days). It then is placed in new, charred American oak barrels where it ages for 5 years, 6 months before it is bottled. But instead of aging in oak barrels, you can fish out a piece of half burned white oak from the fire place, crush it up and place this in the container with your product. Shake it up once a day for about 3 months and then filter it through a coffee filter for a beautiful amber color. Cut it back to 80 or 90 proof for a smooth taste.

The premium brand called Gentlemen J is aged in the same way, with the same grain bill, but it is filtered through maple charcoal again after aging.

Sweetened with a dash of REAL maple syrup (the kind that has a slight smokey flavor)- this will taste JUST like the store bought spirit- but will be a LOT smoother. The spirit should be aged at less than 65%abv, to prevent vanillins from clouding up the smokey sweetness from the maple syrup.

....

STONEWALLS SOUTHERN WHISKEY

One quart of corn syrup per 1 1/2 gallons of water and one cup of honey for every ten

gallon batch. Starting hydrometer reading of about 60 or 65. Do not exceed 70. Add 1 to 3 oz's of yeast per 10 gallons of mash.

Heat one fourth of your water to 120 or 130 degrees only hot enough to melt the corn syrup, then stir in your syrup and then the honey last. Pour it into your fermenter and finish filling with cool water to cool it down to 80 degrees. Take a hydrometer reading and adjust as needed. The add your yeast. 6 to 14 days to ferment.

....

Stonewalls Agave

One 23.5 oz bottle of agave nectar (from the sugar isle at Walmart), to every 3 quarts of water. One 4 oz packet of Turbo yeast for every ten gallon mix. Ferments for 7 to 14 days and distill.

.... Lazy Day Whiskey

INGREDIENTS:

10 lbs. Whole kernel corn, untreated 5 Gallons Water

1.1/3 Cup Yeast,

DIRECTIONS:

Put corn in a burlap bag and wet with warm water. Place bag in a warm dark place and keep moist for about ten days. When the sprouts are about a 1/4" long the corn is ready for the next step. Wash the corn in a tub of water, rubbing

the sprouts and roots off.. Throw the sprouts and roots away and transfer the corn into your primary fermenter. With a pole or another hard object mash the corn, make sure all kernels are cracked. Next add 5 gallons of boiling water

and when the mash cools add yeast. Seal fermenter and vent with a water sealed vent. Fermentation will take 7-10 days. When fermentation is done, pour into still filtering through a pillow case to remove all solids.

.... RYE WHISKEY

INGREDIENTS:

7 Lbs. Rye

2 Lbs. Barley

1 Lbs. Malt

6 gallons of water 1 oz Yeast

DIRECTIONS:

Heat water to 70 degrees and then mix in malt and grain. While stirring the mixture slowly heat to 160 degrees (raise temperature 5 degrees every 2 minutes). Keep mixture at 160 degrees stirring constantly for 2-3 hours to convert starch into fermentable sugar and dextrin. Filter off liquid and place into fermentation device and allow to cool to 70- 80 degrees. Immediately pitch

with 3 grams of yeast. To avoid secondary fermentation and contamination add 1

gram of ammonium-fluoride. Stir liquid for 1 minute then cover and seal with a airlock.Mash will take 5-7 days to ferment. After fermentation is complete pour into, still filtering through a pillow case to remove all solids.

....

GOOD WHISKEY

The ingredients are malt, sugar, yeast and rain water. You can buy the malt from any big supermarket, if they don't have it they will order it for you. The brand names for the malt and yeast I always used was Blue Ribbon, and Red Top. The malt is a liquid and comes in a can, the yeast comes in cakes.

To every can of malt you will add 5 gallons of warm water, dissolve 5 pounds of sugar and add 1 cake of yeast. Mix all this together in a barrel made of plastic, stainless steel, or copper, under no circumstances use aluminum. Keep it covered with cheese cloth to keep the bugs out. Keep it in a warm place till it ferments. Then you can cook it off in your still and you have the smoothest whiskey you have ever tasted.

After you run off the whiskey, it is clear like water. You can color it by taking a piece of dry fruit wood (or maple), burn the fruit wood over a flame till it is blackened real good, then drop the burned fruit-wood in your clear whiskey. In a few days the whiskey will be the color of store bought whiskey.

....

INDIAN HEAD CORN MEAL WHISKEY

Ingredients: 3 Lbs of Indian-Head corn meal

1 1/2- lbs dry malt preferably dark (available at most home-brew shops) 1- sachet of 48 turbo yeast

4- gallons of spring water

After cleaning the equipment to prep it for use, put 3 1/2 gallons of water into the carboy and then slowly add the cornmeal allowing it to wet as it falls to the bottom and thus avoids caking as much as possible.

Carefully lift the carboy and shake it side-to-side to ensure a good mix.

Next add the dry malt like you did the cornmeal,slow and steady and then lift the carboy up and shake it again to get a good mix

Warm the 1/2 gallon of leftover water on the stove until it's just hot to the touch. Turn off the oven and stir in the yeast until it is completely dissolved.

Now add this to the carboy and shake well.

After 3 to 7 days, it's now ready to run off in the still.

....

Ian Smiley's Corn Whisky

20 L water (5 gal)

3.5 kg (8 lb) flaked maize

750 g (1 and 1/2 lb) crushed malted grain

....

. Here is how my late grandfather made ALABAMA CORN WHISKEY:

Take one bushel of untreated seed corn.

Put it in two croaker sacks (burlap bags to any Yankees reading this). Put each sack in a #2 washtub of water at about body temperature.

Weight each sack down with a concrete block. Soak the corn for 12 hours,

Bury the sacks about 4 inches deep in the compost pile.

He had a special compost pile for this. It was composed entirely from oak leaves. When the sprouted corn root is about half the lenght of the corn grain you are ready. Wash the corn in clear water. Grind the corn very course. He used a Corona mill.

Put the ground corn in a 50 gallon wooden barrell. Finish filling the barrell with water. Add 12 packs Fleishmans yeast. Let ferment until complete.

Siphon off the liquor, leaving behind any dead snakes, rats, birds or other varmits. Put it in the still. Fire it off slowly.

If anything came out in under an hour, you are too fast.

Run it through the still 3 times. Catch the first pint of each run. Save it for your Coleman lamp. It ain't fit to drink. That is where your headaches are.

Yield should be about 1 US gallon of pure 100 proff, triple distilled whiskey.

.... To make a grain mash for whiskey : Heat 4 kg cracked or crushed malt with 18 L of water to 63-65 °C, and hold there for 1-1.5 hours. Heat to 73-75 °C, then strain off and keep liquid, using 250 mL of hot water to rinse the grains. Cool to below 30 °C (should have an initial specific gravity of 1.050). Add hydrated yeast & leave to ferment.

To get the same effect, you can also do a malt-extract brew (like making beer kits), then boil 1-2 kg of grains or cracked corn and add them for flavour.

Only use a grain mash if you're specifically after a whisky/bourbon, of if making a vodka and it is cheaper than sugar to do so.

You need to use either malt or enzymes to convert the starch into sugar so that the yeast can use it.\

....

Splash of Irish whiskey

Combine all in a large jar and macerate for a week. Filter trough a coffee filter and ad a

teaspoonful of glucose (dextrose), age for a month or so.

....

Akvavit is mainly used for aperitif, and it is commonly served ice cold from 4cl shot glass. Traditionally there is some salted Baltic herring or smoked salmon served as "sakuski" with it. Another traditional way of serving any type of vodka is that you put a silver coin in bottom of a large cup and pour coffee on it until you can't see it anymore, then pour enough vodka in the cup so that you can see the coin again; drink the whole cupful with one swig...(Warms well in the winter). And, of cause, the real smorgasbord is never complete without an ice-cold bottle of Aquavit...

Wal writes about Poitin...

Quite possibly poitin distillers in the west of Ireland do not have computers so cannot post their recipes to us! Based on background information, together with parallel developments with U.S. moonshine (by Scotch-Irish immigrants) and Russian samogon,

....

Scotch

Soak 50 grams of peated malt in a gallon of water at 155F for 45 minutes- remove the grain, add another gallon and a half of water and bring to a boil- stir in 12 pounds pale malt extract-top up to 5 gallons and cool. Ferment with a dry ale yeast.

Then put this five gallons into 10, half full gallon milk jugs and freeze them SOLID in your freezer. Invert the jars over some one quart canning jars and allow the liquid to drip out (no external heat) until the quart jar is full- the result will be about 2.5 gallons of malt wine at about 17%abv.

Use the "brewing schnapps without a still" type of still (the ice water bath still) to turn this liquid into a 55% abv spirit.

Then blend this unaged spirit 50/50 with some sugar spirit (double distilled and carbon polished- diluted down to 45%abv then aged for one week on virgin-new, uncharred, American oak- 1cup of oak per gallon of spirit) then add one tablespoon of honey per quart bottle (dissolved and boiled until clear in some water- just use equal parts water/honey)

TA DA!!! liquid golden heaven. For a slight fruitiness to this, toss in a raisin or two (per bottle), and let them soak for a week. Having alot of pure sugar spirit around thats really clean tasting is a good thing for anyone (including traditional potstillers') to have laying about! Without blending, pure malt (made with extract) costs about $10US a litre- this makes it more economical, but just as tasty!!

.... "red wax seal" whisky (the founder of the distillery insisted on the Scottish spelling, instead of the Irish "whiskey):

70% corn

14% wheat

16% 6-row barley malt.

Mash in the 150 to 155F range for 90 minutes, then ferment on the grain, strain out the solids, then distill to about 70 to 80%abv. If you have any soured mash (from previous whiskey runs) or "backset" use a mix of backset (33%) and water (67%) for your mashing water- this is how the distillery does it. If you want a more neutral flavor, Stoli vodka is wheat based, just distill an all-wheat mashbill (ferment on the grain again) then distill to a higher proof- around 90%abv.

Chapter2 Sour Mash:

Mashing (holding the temps, etc) is a waste of time for whiskey- the enzymes work in about 90 minutes at mashing temperatures- at room temp, they take about 2 or 3 days (you know, about the same amount of time for a seed to sprout- this is a natural proccess, after all). Because the yeast is in the mix all ready, no time is really lost. As soon as starch converts, it's fermented.

In distilling 'sour mash' is the process of using up to 1/3 of the stillage (ie the grains left after in the wash after fermentation & distilling) in the next batch of mash. The pH is low and it helps save water in the distillery.

(This is different from 'sour-mash' as done by beer brewers, where sour mash is made by allowing lacto baccilus bacteria to lower the pH of the mash before or during ferment. No distiller would ever add lacto or any other bacteria to his mash, for the reason that the bacteria lower the yield of ethanol. If you want to try making a lacto culture take barley malt and soak/cover it with water and let it set for a day or two. You should smell a vinegar aroma, if not, toss it out and try again. Lacto bacillus live on grain)

I have never done it but it is used occasionally in brewing. Some like a sour tang in stouts and Belgian wheat ales. The procedure is very simple. Bring a few handfuls of cracked pale malt in a small mini-mash up to a warm temperature, around 50 °C or so. Hold for a few hours and leave for a couple of days covered with aluminium foil. Some people put it inside a thermos flask to keep the temperature up. The naturally occurring lactobacillus on the grains will multiply and acidify (lactic acid) and sour the malt. It is then added to the main mash. I don't know the theory or practice behind sour mash whisky nor why it is done.

.... "

coming from still residue...

The most explicit is Waymark & Harris _The Book of Classic American Whiskeys_ (although they contain some other inaccuracies) (p. 59 - 60): "Meeting the fresh mash in the fermenting tub is some of the leftover 'distiller's beer' from the lasts distillation.

Called by many names - - thin slop, backset, setback, yeast back - the proportion of this 'yeast back' tends to be around 25 per cent of the total volume of the new mash. The high temperature of the distilling column has taken out the alcohol and killed the yeast, but the leftover spent beer is mildly acidic as a result of the fermentation process. Added to the new mash, the boost in acidity provided by the spent beer inhibits undesired bacteria and yeasts, making the mash - technically, but rarely by distillers, called 'wort' at this stage - safe for the desired distiller's yeast. it also provides a certain continuity in character between batches. It is from this step that we get the term, 'sour mash.' Because of the limestone character of the water, a sweet mash, that is, a mash not using any of the acidic 'yeast back,' would be pH neutral or even a bit alkaline, and hence at high risk of spoilage through undesired microbiological growth."

....

how the sour mash recipe is a variation on the "no-cook" technique :

The reason that modern mashing methods use specifically optimized temperature, pH, water chemistry, etc is to maximize the efficiency of the operation. And, some distillers over the years have argued that such practices over-process the mash and produce a much less natural or desirable flavour.

No-cook recipes have been around for centuries and there are people even today that swear by them. However, a no-cook recipe is very slow and extremely inefficient, and that is why the old-time sour-mash methods were developed, probably about 200 years ago.

The sour-mash method involves the mixing of corn pone (i.e. meal), and other grains such as rye or wheat, with water, and sometimes barley malt, at ambient temperature. Almost all no-cook recipes nowadays involves the addition of sugar as well. A large charge of whiskey yeast is added and a very slow and inefficient fermentation takes place. When the fermentation is complete, the spent grains that float to the top are skimmed off and discarded. The liquid is strained from the mash and distilled into whiskey.

A mixture of about 50% backset (i.e. the left-over liquid in the still after the distillation is finished) and 50% water is added to the remaining grain in the fermenter, and some additional grain is added to make up for what was skimmed off and discarded. There's ample yeast left in the grain sediment in the fermenter so no additional yeast is required. And, a second batch is fermented. When the fermentation is complete, the process is repeated, and so on.

This no-cook sour-mash method is very inefficient by commercial standards, but in the end almost nothing is lost. The same grain and the same liquid (backset) is recycled again and again, with only the spent grains removed. Even the residual alcohol and non- fermentable sugars in the backset is cycled back for another enzyme exposure and fermentation.

....

Sour Mash

One style that is sometimes used for whiskey is that of a "sour mash".

The reason sour mashing is done is to lower the pH of the fermenting mash in order to help prevent bacterial infections. It is used in both rum and bourbon making because both grain and sugar cane/molasses have a large amount of naturally occuring yeast and bacteria growing on them because of the high sugar and starch content these products tend to have. It is much easier (on an industrial scale) to reuse the liquid left in the still after the run is finished to adjust the pH of the next batch, rather than using higher cost food grade acids. It will also help to create a more consistant product from batch to batch.

....

how to do a bourbon/sourmash ...

All the grains you listed (I'd used rye flakes, corn grits & barley flakes but got into trouble) look like a de-husked, pre-processed variety (that will prevent any husk flavors - wheat is (I think) the only grain you can leave in the ferment without worrying about off (tannic) flavors developing. The husk on any other grain will make a drink that tastes like hay horse bedding). It also looks like a bourbon recipe, so, keeping with the industry standard, you ferment on the grain (only malt whiskey is sparged, anything with corn or rye in it is fermented on the grain).

....
Here is how people I know do it.

Mix your grain bill together and weigh it out. For every 3 pounds of grain (1344 grams) you will need one gallon (4 liters) of water.

Put the grain-I use 15 pounds (6.75 Kilos) per 5 gallon (20L) batch- into your fermentor (sanitized, 20+liter buckets are best), pour in 10 liters of room temperature water, and mix it with the grain. Make sure there are no lumps or clumps, and that all the grain has been wetted down (no dry spots are allowed). The first water mixed with the grain MUST NOT BE HEATED!! If it is, the grain will clump together, leaving dry spots in the middle of the clumps, leading to an infection.

Take the next 10 Liters of water and bring it to a boil in a pot on the stove. Once it's boiling, pour it into the bucket with the pre-wetted grain, and stir it up to prevent any clumping. This will liquify the starch, and sanitize the batch (the precooling effects of the grain/water in the bucket will prevent the bucket from warping/melting).

Leave the hot water/grain filled bucket overnight. When cool, add your yeast and your enzyme, and let it ferment. Depending on the grain, when you add the yeast, the mash may be as thick as oatmeal- don't add any more water, it will thin out in a day or so, during the ferment.

Wait until all foaming and bubbling has stopped, and all the grain settles to the bottom (3 days to 2 weeks, depending on temperature), filter this through a layer or two of cheesecloth, and distill it.

.... If you want a true sourmash bourbon, after the distilling of this whiskey, save 4liters of slop from the still (it will be sour after it's been stripped of it's alcohol) and add it to the grain, along with 6 liters of room temp water, instead of just adding 10 liters of cool water. The idea is to get a mix of water/still slop that is 25% still slop (this is the

minimum amount required by law to call the stuff sourmash bourbon in the US). The sour slop will lower the pH dramatically, helping to prevent bacteria, and helping to promote enzyme activity. There you go- no extra equipment needed, and you can fill your fermentor up to just about the top.

.... END OF WHISKEY ....

The Book of: "Rum"

Nefie: "if'n yer don no were yer too, in blind is a bat giffen me screech" English Translation:" please stay out of my moonshine"

Rum

the various recipes ...

The French have two categories of rum - one from the molasses by- product of milling and refining sugar (rhum industriel) and one directly from sugarcane juice (rhum agricole). The 'Household Cyclopedia' of 1881 has a method for making rum which scaled down is about 800 g of molasses/5 litres of water or about 1 l.5 lbs/1 US gal of water. This would give a wash of about 5%abv. To make the equivalent of sugarcane juice, we need 1 cup of white granular sugar, 1/3 cup molasses and 7 cups of water. This would give a sugar content of about 15% which is equivalent to sugarcane juice.

1)   Traditional ('Industrial') Rum (20 l or 5 US gals)

(molasses used in proportion of 1 kg molasses/5 l water) 4 kg (9 lbs) molasses for 20 l (5 US gals) of water

This is equivalent to 100 g sugar/ litre

2)   Traditional ('Industrial') Rum for the Homedistiller (high alcohol) 4 kg molasses and 4 kg white sugar for 20 l water

This is equivalent to 300 g sugar/litre

3)   'Agricultural' Rum (French rhum agricole, Brazilian cachaca) 3 kg white sugar and 1 kg molasses for 20 l of water (17% sugar) This is equivalent to 175 g sugar/litre

4)   'Agricultural' Rum for the Homedistiller (high alcohol)

5.5 kg white sugar and 1.5 kg molasses for 20 l water This is equivalent to 310 g sugar/litre

Rum gets additional flavor from ex Bourbon barrels and caramelised (burnt) sugar. A suggested proportion would be 5-10 tsp/litre of rum which would give a sweetness of 2.5- 5% which is in line with what is added to other liquors.

use a 7L pot still with thumper so I have to make 3 runs per batch (you just can't argue with free). It comes off at 75-80%. My wash is made from about 8kg cheap brown sugar and 50g yeast nutrient in 23L bucket, it finishes at about 15% alc using champagne yeast. I found that aging in toasted oak for at least a week, undiluted, made a product that would fool my friends. Noticed an even grater improvement when I got lazy and didn't discard my oak chips and just added more. Great taste when diluted to about 45%.

The foreshots are easy. Even with a 7-8L batch I discard the first 50-60mL. I stop collecting when the temp. off the thumper reaches about 185 F (85C). I notice that at this point % alc. begins to fall as well and the smell changes.I still keep going till the temp off the still reaches about 195 F (90.5C)

I have found a quick way to make charred oak chips. I wrap a tinfoil packet of oak chips about 3 layers and put them on my stove element at less than medium... Here's what keeps the fire out, a big old iron frying pan placed on top. In about 1/2 hr. good Smokey oak. I also sometimes add some caramelized brown sugar if the batch seems a bit harsh.

....
BLACK BEARDS RUM

Two pounds of brown sugar per one gallon of water and one cup of honey for every ten gallon batch. Starting hydrometer reading of about 90. Do not exceed 100. Add 1 to 3 ozs of yeast per 10 gallons of mash.

Heat one fourth of your water to 120 or 130 degrees only hot enough to melt the sugar, then stir in your sugar and then the honey last. Pour it into your fermenter and finish filling with cool water to cool it down to 80 degrees. Take a hydrometer reading and adjust as needed. The add your yeast. 6 to 14 days to ferment.

....
1842 recipe for poitin (pronounced Pah-cheen)

boil 5 gallons of water and pour it over a mix of ten pounds of rolled oats (unflavored oatmeal) that has had a pound of 6 row barley (ground) and mixed in to it.

Allow this to sit until it is cool enough to add yeast, then add a dry ale yeast and 15 drops of liquid beano (or three of the pills). When you add the yeast/Beano enzyme to the cooled mash the stuff may be thick - like stiff oatmeal- don't worry. The yeast breaks it down with the beano as it is fermenting. Within a day it will be a liquid with grain floating in it.

ferment until dry

double distill in a potstill. Don't age drink it white.

From what I have read, oat whiskey is the ONLY spirit to have totally died off.. The last commercial distillery was in Ireland- and it shut down in 1975. Oats are a relatively expensive grain, as well as being very sticky, so distillers don't like it very much. If it is filtered well, and run on a water-bath still (or an ice water/wok still) there should be no problem

....

1)   Single Malt Poitin

(This would be the original raw 'uisce beatha' before cognac aging techniques were adapted. Prior to this cognac method, dried fruits were used to provide flavor)

20 litres water (5 U.S. gal)

5 kg (10 lb) crushed malted barley grain Yeast (preferably beer yeast)

Barley is malted by soaking and spreading out in a 25 mm (1 in) layer to sprout. Wait until sprouts ('acrospires') are 5 mm long. You can then use this 'green malt' immediately by crushin lightly and adding to water at 65C (149F) for a 90 minute conversion rest. Leave to cool to fermentation temperature of 24C. Add yeast. (It is possible to harvest yeast from the sediment in bottle conditioned Australian or Belgian beer.)

....

Canadian Spiced Rum

800 mL 80% rum (fermented from 6kg brown sugar, 25gm citric acid [to invert the sugar] , 25gm Supervit (Italian) yeast nutrient. 10gm Ec-1118 yeast from Lalvin (ferments HIGH ALCOHOL!!!) Run this stuff through a good reflux coloumn.

1/4-tsp ground cloves

1/4-tsp (generous) powdered cinnamon 1/4-tsp (generous) powdered ginger

1-tsp-Crosby's Cooking Molasses (Blackstrap will do !)

1-Tbsp-Toasted White Oak Chips (Check your local wine shop as this is a popular addition to Red WIne !)

Now....after all this CRAP   let this stuff macerate in a 60 oz (1.7L) bottle (plastic or

glass   your choice) for at least 7 (SEVEN) DAY'S (PLEASE!!!). SHAKE-THE-CRAP-

OUTTA-THIS-BOTTLE-EVERY-DAY for the whole week (make's the flavours blend incredibly well). If you want an even fuller flavour leave the bottle (or bottles) to

macerate (soak) for another week.   (let's the spices and stuff impart an even stronger

flavour). Play with it   see what you like!!

After this   you must run your (YUMMY-STUFF) through a coffee filter 2 (TWO) times

at least (more filtering. clearer product!!!).

After this   you must top off the bottle (SORRY) to the top!!! This will give you about

38% alc/vol   which is perfect for this type of rum. I know that the Captain Morgan Rum

is 3% less in alcohol   and it is much sweeter.

6kg blackstrap molasses 1 pkt yeast nutrient

1 pkt lalvin EC1118 3kg white sugar

In a 25litre fermenter with air lock, disolve the molasses and nutrient in warm water to around 22 litres at 25degC, pitch the yeast and keep the temp around 25degC until all bubbling stops. Add the 3kgs of sugar giving a quick stir and let it go at 25degC and leave for a couple of days after bubbling finishes. Decant, leaving the sediment behind (save the sediment in a sterile jar for the next batch).

When you distill, drop something in the boiler to aid bubbling when it boils (I use a couple of copper pipe offcuts (about 1"x1") to stop surging and give it just enough heat to do the job.

Throw out the first 50mls and collect the rest to about 88 to 90degC. I pull it off at about 80%.

Toast some american white oak in alfoil until smokin, let cool, then mix with the rum with about 2 tablespoons of golden syrup (cocky's joy, treacle) and 1 tablespoon of food grade molasses for every 2ltrs of rum for about 4 to 5 days. Filter through a coffee filter

and water down to 40% (80 proof) and enjoy.

Don't forget to shake the bottle every day while on oak.

....

light rum/neutral spirit recipe

15 lbs (6.8 kg) white sugar

24 oz molasses

5 tbsp yeast nutrient 2 tsp yeast energizer

yeast starter (see below)

To make yeast starter: Dissolve 4 tbsp Red Star brand Distiller's Yeast in 3 cups water at 93-97 degrees F (34-36C). Add 1 tbsp molasses, and 2 tbsp white sugar. Stir or shake until disolved and cover. Let sit, shaking occasionally for 1/2 hour to 1 hour.

Heat 1 gal (4L) water to almost boiling, pour into fermentor. Disolve 10 lbs sugar, molasses, yeast nutrient, and yeast energizer into hot water. Top up to 6 Gallons (23L) with cold water keeping temperature at 85- 89 degrees F (29-32C). Stir until well mixed. Pour yeast starter into fermentor and stir briskly. Put lid and air lock on fermentor.

After a few minutes, the ailock should start bubbling briskly. Keep wort at 85 degrees F (29C) for the duration of fermentation.

When you have a mixture of liquids, each with its own boiling point when pure, then the boiling point of the mix will lie somewhere in the middle, and this will depend on the relative concentrations of each liquid. Pure water boils at 100 deg C, and pure ethanol boils at 78.5 deg C, but a mixture of water and ethanol will boil at some point in between. The major point about distillation is that when a mixture like that boils, then the vapour given off is richer in the most volatile component, and when that vapour condenses then the resulting liquid has a lower boiling point than the mix it came from. By repeating this boiling and recondensation process up a column, using packing to hold the condensed liquid at each stage, you can separate the components more and more.

So if you have a mixture of liquids each with a different boiling point, then you heat the mixture, it will heat up until the new intermediate boiling point is reached. When you first start a distilling run, the packing in the column will be at room temperature, so vapour given off by the boiler condenses on the first cool packing it reaches. In condensing, the vapour gives up a lot of heat, and this warms that packing until the liquid on it boils again. However, this liquid is richer in volatiles than the mix in the boiler, so its boiling point is lower. When it does boil again, from the heat given off by more condensing vapour, what you get is even richer in those most volatile components. This process of boiling and condensing continues up the column and, because the condensed liquid is always getting richer in volatiles, the temperature gradually falls the higher you go. The temperature at any point is governed solely by the boiling point of that liquid mix, and any attempt to interfere with that process will disrupt the separation that Nature is carrying out automatically.

In contrast, the boiling point of the mix left in the boiler will very slowly start to rise as it is left with less and less of the most volatile components.

If you started with a mixture (fermented wash) that is mostly water & ethanol, with trace amounts of methanol, propanol, etc. then the net result will be that the most volatile components will tend to rise in greater quantity up the column than their less volatile cousins, and will be found in greatest concentration at the top. This would mean that methanol, the most volatile of the lot, will win the race and you will able to collect it and set it aside. This continues until you have collected all of the "heads" (components that are more volatile than ethanol), and you can then collect just ethanol with a trace of water. You cannot get rid of that small amount of water, as once you reach a mix of 96.5% ethanol/water, with a boiling point of 78.2 deg C, then you have reached a stable mix that no amount of re-boiling and re-condensation can change (at normal atmospheric pressure).

Once you have collected the main bulk of ethanol, then the components that are less volatile than ethanol, such as propanol and the bigger organic molecules, will start to reach the top, and you will have arrived at the stage called the "tails". These "tails" may be recycled in the next batch you do, for they still contain a lot of ethanol, or a proportion may be retained as they contain many of the compounds that give a spirit a distinctive flavour, like whiskey or rum.

Note that you are not changing any part of your original brew - you're not "making" the alcohol, or converting it to something else or nasty. All you are doing is concentrating off the original brew into its various parts. There is no more methanol after you finish than what you started with. What does happen though, is that because most of the methanol comes off at once (first up), it is highly concentrated, and can damage you. You definitely don't want to be sampling the first portion of distillate that you collect. But once you have thrown away this part, you have guaranteed that the remaining distillate is safe enough to partake of.

....

2)   Grain Poitin

You only need about 10% malted barley grain to provide the enzymes to convert starch to

fermentable sugars. According to the literature rye, oats and wheat were used. About 1-

1.5 kg (2-3 lb)/4 l (5 US gal) is used.

....

Poteen

20 l water

450 g bakers yeast 3 kg brown sugar

250 g treacle (molasses)

65 g hops Steep ingredients in 2 litres of lukewarm water. Add additional cold water and then add the yeast and ferment for several weeks. Transfer to still.

....

'Beercommie' "Poteen is Irish moonshine, it is pronounced 'pocheen', and is usually made from grain, barley, wheat, or rye. I'm not ruling out potato, but its safe to say that potato is not the fermentable of choice."

....

'Fintan Swanton' "Poitin (literally 'little pot', meaning the still in which the drink is made) is an illicit spirit made from just about anything which comes to hand - grain, potatoes, or probably commonest these days, just yeast and sugar."

.... Old Protrero recipe:

Mash 100% rye malt at 110F for 30minutes, then 145 (30minutes), then 155 (30minutes) to get the best conversion, then cool with a wort chiller to 80F and add your yeast. (if you wonder about water chemistry, use the kind for "California common" styles of beer)

The 110F rest is called a "beta-glucan" rest- it is done to break up the gums in malted and unmalted grain, and in beer brewing can increase sugar yields by as much as 15%.

Double distilling in a potstill (collect the run in separate lots, say 100ml, and blend them together by taste) is what is done for Old Protrero (they use an old fashioned alembic style still- it looks like a onion-topped Cognac still).

It is aged for just about one year in UNCHARRED American oak barrels- he did this to allow the peppery/honey quality of the rye to come through more strongly than the vanillins from charred oak, plus, he admits to trying to replicate an early 1800's whiskey, and charred barrels were not required in America until 1933- he ("he" being Fritz

Maytag- the founder of the distillery, and founder/owner of the Anchor Steam brewery) is also experimenting with some new charred oak for his later runs- but I don't think any has been released

…………………………………………… END OF RUM …………………………………

The Book of: "Vodka"

A reporter goes way up into the hills of West Virginia to write an article about the area. He meets an old man in a small town and asks him about any memorable events in his life.

The old man says, "Well, one time my favorite sheep got lost, so me and my neighbors got some moonshine and went looking for it. We looked and looked and finally found the sheep. Then we drank the moonshine and one by one, started shagging the sheep. It was a lot of fun!"

The reporter figured he can't write an article about that, so he asked the old man to tell him another story.

The old man said, "Well, one time my neighbor's wife got lost, so me and all the village men got some moonshine and went out looking for her. We looked and looked and finally we found her. Then we drank the moonshine and one by one, started shagging the neighbor's wife. Now, THAT was a lot of fun!"

The reporter, feeling frustrated, finally told the old man that he couldn't write articles about those stories and asked him if he had any dramatic or sad memories that he could talk about.

The old man paused a little and with a sad expression on his face said - "Well, one time I was lost..."

Chapter1 History of Vodka

I have formed the opinion that early poitin was raw single (barley) malt whiskey. Peat

was the heat source. Later to cut costs (possibly in line with Scottish practice) malted barley and other grains (wheat, oats, rye)were used. The use of treacle (molasses) is mentioned, as is raw (brown) sugar, (one source says sugar was used after 1880).

Currently barley and sugar, or even sugarbeet pulp is mentioned. I would imagine if potatoes were not suitable for eating, that they would be used too. Potatoes, were once an essential staple in the Irish diet (in 1845, consumption was 5 kg/day), and even now 140 kg/head/year are consumed. 1 acre could feed a family for a year. Larger farms grew grain that was used as a cash crop. It is all a matter of convenience and economics. I doubt whether potatoes were used before the 1900's the time they became the principal source for vodka in Estonia. A similar story is seen with U.S. moonshine and Russian samogon. The Irish pot still and the Scottish pot still are similar and have basically simplified the geometry of the alchemist's alembic still. A similar shape is often seen in the U.S.probably brought over by Celtic immigrants.

It is often said that the 'exise free' Irish poitin (poteen) is made from potatoes. Home distillation is still a word-of-mouth tradition in Ireland and I have not been able to find actual recipes for poitin, but I picked up some interesting clues.

Potatoes were actually introduced by Sir Walter Raleigh onto his plantation in Cork in 1589, and quickly became a staple in the Irish diet. But was it fermented and distilled? In Poland, until the 18th century, vodka was produced chiefly from rye, wheat, barley and oats. Johann Joachim Becher developed a method of producing spirits from potatoes in 1669, but it was not until 1798 that the first instructions for "a practical way of distilling

vodka from potatoes" was published. Distillers did not begin to use potatoes on a large scale until 1820. The potato is a relatively expensive source for alcohol. Potatoes contain 15-18% fermentable material while grains contain 50-67%. 10 kg of potatoes produce 1 litre of alcohol while 10 kg of grain produces 4 litres. Because of the 1845-1849 Famine in Ireland, some 1 million people died and some 1 million people emigrated. The immigrants to the U.S.A. brought their distilling knowledge with them but they did not use the potato, preferring the native maize. This suggest that a poitin made from potatoes is a late innovation and it is more than likely this began after 1900

....

Russian Vodka (Samogon)

I was under the impression that vodka was made from unmalted grain until I came across a Russian language site: http://www.stopka.ru/drink/samogon/samogon00.shtml.The

site gives instructions for making a simple pot still and a Chinese still (using a central wok- like condenser), and samogon recipes.

....

Using Potatoes

For those of you interested in making authentic Vodka or Schnapps from potato. The problem with potatoes (as all starchy vegetables) is the need to first break down the starch into basic sugars so that the yeast can use them. This is done by using enzymes, either via malted grains or from a packet
there are probably better instructions and

details in books on Schnapps of which in English there is a real dearth of. I would imagine there are some very good books available in German. What I have described is basically the process for saccharifying barley which applies to all grains as long as sufficient enzymes are added and the starch chains are not too long or complex. Barley has by far the highest % of natural amalase (diastase) enzymes plus a very high starch content of a fairly simple nature which is more readily broken down than most grains hence its widespread use and popularity from the ancient Summerians and Egyptians to the current day.

The advantage of potatoes over most grains is the amount of starch that can be produced per acre (up to 80 tons per hectare with the world record being about 120 ton. Note wet weight not actual starch content although this is generally 80% + of its dry weight). Its disadvantage is the lack of enzymes which must be added (until 40 or 50 years ago not fully understood). I believe the only one that can equal potaoes is cassava (tapioca) but you need a tropical climate to grow it. Traditionally these have been processed at lower temperatures and left soaking for quite a reasonable time, basically to give the enzymes time to do their job and to save energy I would imagine.

I suspect the reason Simons first attempt failed was largely because of insufficient amalase enzymes. Temperature possibly also had a small bearing.

I would imagine there is not that much difference in basic processing of schnapps and vodka both being identical in the initial processing although I have not done a lot of reading on the matter.

To get this better we really need to know the proper composition of potatoe starch and its

liquefaction and saccharification temps. Somewhere I have some general details on these last two especially liquefaction but todate do not have accurate details on starch composition. I believe the Danes have done quite a bit of work and reasearch on this aspect (composition).

Potatoes are harder than most people think and you need a bit of experience to get them right. Books make it sound so easy because they tend to simplify the process and take for granted that you have a full understanding and experience of all the steps involved quite often leaving out some of the elementary steps. Most of us need to fully understand the basics first before we really begin to learn. I have not tried potatoes yet myself but know this from my reading, broad experiernce of other aspects, and experience with other forms of starch.

What you will probably need to do is what is called a Stepped Infusion Mash. This is where you start the saccharification process at a low temperature and then move it up in steps, halting for a certain time period at each step to give each enzyme time to break down as much as they can at each stage. If you have made beer in the past using an all- grain mash you will understand the process.

To get a feeling for it and to understand the process better try the following:

Cook your potatoes so they are still stiff - about 12- 15 minutes at reasonable heat. Up to 20 minutes at low heat. Note they should still be a bit undercooked, definitely not soft, mushy, or floury.

Add coarsely milled barley (particles mostly about 1/16 to 3/32" in size. Definitely not too fine.). Use malted Ale barley or standard malted barley rather than Lager barley as it is definitely higher in enzymes and enzymatic action. Note you need sprouted malted barley not spray-dried malt which is normally on a maltodextrin base and has had most of the enzymes destroyed or inactivated because of the excessive heat used in the drying process.

Cover with sufficient water and bring to 113 F (45 C). Hold 15 minutes stirring regularly. Bring up to 133 F (56 C). Hold 15 minutes etc.

Bring up to 149 F (65 C). Hold 15 minutes stirring constantly.

Bring up to 158 F (70 C). Hold 15 minutes stirring constantly. All up this makes 60 minutes which should suffice for a small batch. Some batches will take longer especially bigger batches. Most of the liquifaction and saccharification occurs in steps 5 & 6 rather than 3 & 4. If you want to alter this reduce 3 & 4 to 10 minutes and increase 5 & 6 to 20 minutes or longer where required.

Once virtually all the starch is liquified and broken down to simple sugars to halt the enzymatic process raise the temp to 176 F (80 C) (Mashing Out) and then drop it back as quickly as possible to between 140 F (60 C) and 122 F (50 C) so the sugars dont get scorched or burnt.

Cool down further to 75 F (24 C), establish an SG of 1060 (min) to 1080 (max = ideal) and begin fermentation.

If you muck around with the basic formula doing several batches, altering the temperature and times a small amount each time you will quickly get a feel for it and learn far more than you can learn initially out of books or I can spell out for you.

I suggest you start with 3 or 4 kg of potatoes and 1/2 kg of barley each time so you have plenty of enzymes together with a very large pot so it dosnt boil over. Once you have got this basic process under control and gained a bit of experience I can help you further with advice and help with enzymes. Also once you have the experience and understand fully what you are doing with the right selection of enzymes you can reduce this 4 to 5 steps down to 2 or 3 steps and save a lot of energy and time producing virtually the same result.

At first for the small amount produced it hardly seems worthwhile but you will be amazed at how quickly you have control of the process with a bit of experience. Learn this process properly now and it will save you a lot of time later.

The most important enzymes are Alpha amylase, Gluco amylase and to minor extent Beta amylase. Beta has largely been replaced by Gluco. The other important factor is temperature with each of these working best (most active) at certain temperatures. Alpha works best at higher temperatures normally chopping the starch into smaller blocks whereas Gluco and Beta work from the ends. Temperatures required of the process are therefore dependant on makeup and complexity of the starch.

As mentioned without knowing the exact composition of the potatoe starch I cannot advise exactly the necessary temps and times. The setup I have given you is basically for barley but should work quite satisfactory with potatoes because of the range of temperatures involved.

What I am saying here applies to barley as well as individual enzymes. The heat of cooking the potatoes will start the process. For all I know it may help to throw a handful of barley in with the potatoes when you begin cooking. Keep good notes of amounts, times, and temps and if you have much better success compared to the last time or another batch you should be quickly able to repeat it. By doing this you will quickly get a good idea of what is required. Keep me up todate with how you get on.

Be aware that enzymes are protein and bio-catalyst and like other proteins consist of long chains of amino acids held together by peptide chains. They are present in all living cells where they perform a vital function by controlling the metabolic processes and hence the breakdown of food into simpler compounds eg. Amylases break down starch into simple sugars. As bio-catalyst by their mere presence and without being consumed in the process they can speed up chemical processes that would otherwise run very slowly being released at the end of the process to begin it all again if required. In theory this can go on forever but in practice they have a limited stability and over a period of time they lose their activity because of variables particularly temperature changes and are not useable again. In practice therefore be very wary of quickly changing and wildly fluctuating temperatures.

Akvavit -The Scandinavian flavored vodka.

The most famous flavored vodka from Scandinavia is probably Akvavit (or Aquavit if

you ask from any Dane.) Akvavit is not actually vodka, it is just specially made grain based spirit flavoured with caraway seeds and sometimes aged with oak. Most fanciest type of Aquavit, the Norwegian "Linie Aquavit" even travels in oak barrels on a ship from Australia and back, just for getting the special flavor... Other well-known brands are the Danish "Aalborg" and the "Aalborgs Jubilæums Aquavit".

....

Akvavit has quite long roots, the oldest recipe that I found is dated back to year 1642, this is a Finnish recipe is from year 1802, and this is how it goes (converted for home distilling purposes):

1   kg of barley flour 1 kg of oat flour

2	kg of rye flour

5 kg of cooked and smashed potatoes 5 kg of gristed rye malt

about 30 L of water

15L of sour mash (from previous batch) or 20g of citric acid and 10l of water couple of juniper branches

½ L of beer sediment

Clean linen cloth and some rope 50 - 70L bucket

100 g of coarsely chopped caraway seeds

500 g of powdered charcoal (made from birch if available) 20 g of coriander seeds

10 g of dill

Couple handfuls of washed sand

Cotton bag, big enough to hold all these Copper or silver coin

Large bottle (and optionally some oak (and sandalwood) chips)

Put the grains and potatoes in the bucket and soak in the sour mash for couple of hours. Boil the juniper branches in 30litres of water; remove the branches and pour the boiling water on the grains and potatoes and stir well. Leave there over night, and in the morning check the temperature (must be 20 - 27 degrees Celsius) and add beer sediment (or about 50g of ale/porter yeast). Stir. Cover the bucket with the linen cloth and secure tight with rope. (You'll see why in a day or two). Let ferment until there is about 10cm (4") deep layer of clear liquid on the top (this should take about two weeks or so). Distill in a water/steam bath pot still (with the tails from previous batch) three times (just like you were making Irish-type whiskey).

Fill the still with the middle run from third distillation and put the coin in the still. Fill the cotton bag in the following order: first put sand in the bag, enough to cover the bottom of the bag. Then put the spices (caraway seeds, coriander and dill) in the bag. Mix the charcoal and the remaining sand and put in the top of the bag. Hang the bag below the stills outlet tube, so that the distillate can drop through the bag to the receiving container. Distill slowly; the heat input to the still is correct when the coin rattles about once in a second (col... col... col...). Collect until the tails show up. Cut the distillate down to 50vol.% with spring water (use bottled water if you can't obtain fresh spring water) and

age in the glass bottle at least for two months. (Add couple of oak (and sandalwood) chips if available).

....

Simplified recipe (of my own invention)

4   L of 40 vol.% vodka (or well made Moonshine...) 30 g of caraway seeds

5 g of coriander seeds 5 g of dryed dill Some oak chips

.... END OF Vodka ....

The Book of: "Gin"

What is Bathtub Gin?

Few people have ever had proper bathtub gin and most would probably would not ever want to. Regular gin is a redistillation of neutral grain alcohol with certain botanicals such as juniper berries, citrus peepls, anis or orris root. Bathtub gin, created in the days of America's Prohibition of alcohol is a crude version of this recipe that was in private homes for consumption in hidden backrooms and speakeasies. Gin was chosen because, unlike whiskey, it didn't need to age for long so it could be ready to drink very quickly.

But, despite the name, bathtub gin wasn't made in a bathtub. Instead it was made by steeping grain alcohol with juniper berries and water in a large jar too large to be filled in a sink, hence it was filled from the bathtub tap. However, because distilling was illegal during the Prohibition, denatured alcohol was used when grain alcohol wasn't available, which led to illness, blindness or death in many cases. Even with the botanical flavorings, bathtub gin was notoriously dry and had a foul taste. Many modern cocktails were designed to mask the taste of bathtub gin.

Making Crude Bathtub Gin

Today, the term is used loosely for any amateur distilled spirits, like moonshine. Still, making an authentic, but relatively safe, rendition of good old bathtub gin is not very difficult. In absolutely no circumstance should rubbing alcohol, mineral spirits or any other form of denatured alcohol be used. Instead, for a rustic flavor, combine equal parts water and strong grain alcohol in a sealable container. Add to this about 10 grams of dried juniper berries and two grams of orange or lemon peel per 750 mL of liquid. Cover the jar and store in a cool, dark place for two days to one week depending on how much flavor you want to infuse. Shake thoroughly once each day. When the mixture is uncovered, pass through a strainer for a sample of the iconic drink of the roaring twenties. You'll probably want to mix it with cranberry or some other juice to help it go down.

.... A Modern Twist

Grain alcohol, of course, is not exactly known for its refined taste. Bootleggers used it because they didn't have the time to properly distill alcohol and it was more risky and expensive for them to do so. You, on the other hand, have no reason to put yourself through that experience when you have the advantage of dozens of well-crafted vodkas you can work with. The best idea is to start with a bottle of your favorite vodka, preferable one that has a 100-proof variety. Follow a similar process as the recipe above, but don't hesitate to experiment with different botanicals--in addition to the juniper berries, why not try some cardamom, cloves, nutmeg or Thai basil? Another recommendation is to use a reliable water filter to get any residual cloudiness out of the concoction.

....

Bathtub Gin Recipe from Aunt Karen

. Use a scale as some of the measurements are pretty subtle. What I used:

1/2 ounce fresh cilantro, use stems and leaves, and weigh before washing and drying 3/8 ounce lemon or lime peel, use a vegetable peeler to remove just the peel (we used Meyer and Bears for the two batches; the color of the citrus is what mostly colors the alcohol; the Meyer lemon peel above photographed a little orange but it was in fact a super deep yellow)

3 grams fresh marjoram leaves, use no stems (2 lightly packed tablespoons) 14 to 16 juniper berries, available at health food stores and specialty markets

2 to 4 green cardamom pods, crushed (use more if you like cardamom's menthol qualities)

10 white peppercorns 2 1/2 teaspoons sugar

8 1/2 fluid ounces vodka (we used Smirnoff)

3 3/8 fluid ounces Trebianno white wine (a nearly bone dry Italian white wine typically used for blending; it's known as Ugni Blanc in France)

Put all the ingredients in a small saucepan. Heat over medium-high heat until bubbles appear at the edge. Lower the heat to medium and put the timer on for 2 minutes. This opens up the aromatics.

Turn off the heat, transfer everything to a quart-size glass jar and cap. Leave it to steep at room temperature for 18 to 24 hours. Strain through a paper coffee filter. The gin is ready to drink.

....

Gin

Single Grain

20 l water (5 US gal)

4 kg (9 lb) crushed and cooked grain (barley, rye, oats, wheat)
500 g (1 lb) crushed malted barley grain

Yeast

....

b) Mixed Grain

20 l water (5 US gal)

2 kg (4 and 1/2 lb) crushed malted barley grain

1.5 kg (3 lb)crushed barley grain (cooked) 250 g (1/2 lb) crushed
oats (cooked)

250 g (1/2 lb) crushed rye grain (cooked) 250 g (1/2 lb) crushed
wheat grain (cooked) Yeast

....

3)   Sugar and Treacle 20 l water (5 US gal)

3 kg (61/2 lb) brown sugar

250 g (1/2 lb) treacle (molasses) 65 g (2 oz) hops

450 g (1 lb) bakers yeast

Steep ingredients in 2 l (1 qt) of lukewarm water. Add additional
cold water and yeast.

....

b) Mixed Grain

20 l water (5 US gal)

2 kg (4 and 1/2 lb) crushed malted barley grain

1.5 kg (3 lb)crushed barley grain (cooked) 250 g (1/2 lb) crushed oats (cooked)

250 g (1/2 lb) crushed rye grain (cooked) 250 g (1/2 lb) crushed wheat grain (cooked) Yeast

....

Single Grain

20 l water (5 US gal)

4 kg (9 lb) crushed and cooked grain (barley, rye, oats, wheat) 500 g (1 lb) crushed malted barley grain

Yeast

....

4)   Grain and Sugar 20 l water (5 US gal)

4 kg (9 lb) crushed barley (cooked) 500 g (1lb) crushed malted barley grain 2 kg (4 and 1/2 lb) sugar

Yeast

1 kg of grain is equivalent to about 600 g of sugar. Beer yeast would ferment out about a maximum of 5 kg(10 lb) sugar/20 l (5 US gal) of water, so you can juggle the proportions to suit.

.... END OF GIN ....

The Book of: "Fruit & Grain"

Fruit

WATERMELON-PEACH MOONSHINE BRANDY for five gallons 1 1/4 large watermelon

10 peaches

1 1/4 cup chopped golden raisins 15 limes (juice only)

25 cups sugar

water to make 5 gallon wine or distillers yeast

Extract the juice from watermelon and peaches, saving pulp. Boil pulp in five quarts of water for 1/2 hour then strain and add water to extracted juice. Allow to cool to lukewarm then add water to make five gallons total and all other ingredients except yeast to primary fermentation vessel. Cover well with cloth and add yeast after 24 hours. Stir daily for 1 week and strain off raisins. Fit fermentation trap, and set aside for 4 weeks.

....

WATERMELON-ELDERBERRY MOONSHINE BRANDY

32 Lb watermelon

1 1/4 Lb dried elder-berries water to 5 gallon

juice and zest of 10 lemons 36 cups granulated sugar wine or distillers yeast

Cut the rind off of melon, cut melon into one-inch cubes, remove loose seeds, and put melon and any free juice in primary (crock, plastic pail, etc.). Grate the yellow thinly off ten lemons, then juice the lemons and add the juice and zest (gratings) to primary. Add dried elderberries. Add water to make up 5 gallons. Stir in sugar and stir well to dissolve. Cover primary with cloth, wait 12 hours and add yeast. Cover and ferment 3 days, stirring daily. Strain juice into secondary (demijohn) and fit airlock. Ferment 30 days.

....

WATERMELON-GRAPE MOONSHINE BRANDY

30 Lb watermelon

7-1/2 Lb fresh table red or green grapes water to 5 gallon

juice and zest of 10 lemons 24 cups granulated sugar wine or distillers yeast

Cut the rind off of melon, cut melon into one-inch cubes, remove loose seeds, and put melon and any free juice in primary (crock, plastic pail, etc.). Thinly grate the yellow off ten lemons, juice the lemons, and add the juice and zest (gratings) to primary. Separately, wash, destem, and crush the grapes well in a bowl. Add grapes and grape juice. Add water to make up 5 gallon. Add sugar and stir well to dissolve. Cover primary with cloth, wait 24 hours. Add yeast. Cover and ferment 5 days, stirring dairy. Strain juice into secondary (demijohn) and fit airlock. Ferment 30 days.

....

WELCHES FROZEN GRAPE JUICE MOONSHINE BRANDY

10 cans (11.5 oz) Welches 100% frozen grape concentrate 7 Lbs granulated sugar

water to make 5 gallons wine or distillers yeast

Bring 5 quarts of water to boil and dissolve the sugar in the water. Remove from heat and add frozen concentrate. Add additional water to make five gallons and pour into secondary. Add remaining ingredients except yeast. Cover with cloth fastened with rubber band and set aside 12 hours. after cooling to proper yeast temperature, add activated yeast and recover with cloth. Ferment 30 days..

....

APPLE PIE BRANDY.

Heat one gallon of apple juice. Do not exceed 150 degrees.

Add one cup of honey, 2 tsp of cinnamon oil and 2 tsp of nutmeg. Stir until dissolved.

Let this mixture cool down to room temperature and add one fifth of either rum, vodka of shine. Rum is best.

Put into jars and let set for two weeks. Moonshine

A "genuine" moonshine recipe, as still being used by Deb Brewer is ...

5 gallon bucket all grain horse feed (we use MannaPro Hi Grain sweet feed)

one package of yeast (using bread yeast now--others will increase quality and ferment time)

5 pounds sugar water

Put enough feed to cover bottom of 5 gallon bucket a good 4 inches deep Add 5 pounds of sugar. Fill 1/2 full with warm water--warm enough to melt sugar but not so hot as to kill yeast. Mix until sugar is dissolved. Add yeast and mix some more finish filling with warm water--again not so hot to kill the yeast. Cover with lid--our lid has a little cap that screws on, leave it loose to breathe.

.... 4-5 days later it's ready to run! This is an old-timer recipe and works quite well. Our liquor is always 170-190 proof. You can substitute corn meal for the grain but I don't

recommend this for pot stills cuz you can't filter it well enough. The meal will settle and burn in the bottom of your still. The old-fashion way of making corn liquor--with real corn--just is not feasible time wise.

the only way I can tell you is by the barrel full. We used 55 gal. barrels or 53 gal. oak whiskey barrels. Take 100 lb. of cracked yellow corn (this corn needs to be air dried, not dried by gas, gas dried takes the goodies out of it) Put the meal in the barrel, put about 40 gal. of good water in your cooker and heat the water to about 100 degrees, drain the water by the bucket full and stir your sugar in so it dissolves good, we used 50 lbs. sometimes 60 lbs. of sugar on the first barrel.

Here's probley whats different, we DID NOT add any YEAST of any kind to this. If the weather is in the mid 90's this would work off in 5 to 7 days, about day 2 or 3 it sounded like Rice Crispie's that just had milk poured over them, agin no yeast was added. We did take a wood paddle and maybe stir it once or twice a day. In those days all there was available was baker's yeast, and adding baker's yeast caused an off taste, hic-ups, indigestion or heartburn so thats why it was left out. In cold weather sometimes yeast was used to get the first barrel going.

When the mash got "dog heads" on it, that's when the large single bubbles come about

20-30 seconds apart it was ready to cook off, its better to cook a day early than a day late. The mash also had a sour taste to it. On a 50 or so gal. cooker with two propane burners, shine would start running in about an hour. The cooling barrel was also about 55 gal. with a 5/8 inch by 40 foot copper worm, had cold water running in the top and discharging water coming out mid ways or most time at the bottom of the barrel. This first run would usually start at about 120-125 proof and let it run down to about 80 proof, this was strained through a heavy white felt hat, sometimes a double hand full of hickory charcoal was used in the hat also. You put this 80-125 proof to side to keep, but kept running from the 80 proof on down to about 45-50 proof, this would be about a gal.and we called it singles. The 80-125 proof would be about 4 gal.

You cut your cooker off when you got to the 45-50 proof and let the beer cool down to about 100 degrees. You took about 3, 3lb. coffee cans of your meal out of the barrel and put the same amount of fresh back in (this makes a difference in your next yield and proof) mix another 60 lbs of sugar to your warm beer and put back in your mash barrel and stir up, let it work off agin.

On your 2nd run, put your beer in the cooker and also the gal. of singles you saved out. This run here should start out about 135 proof, have seen it go to 140, after a gal or so it may be 120 and stay 120 for an hour or better before it drops lower in proof, this run usally last about 2 1/2-3 hours and makes about 9 gal. agin quit saving it when it gets to 80 proof but keep running till down to the 45-50 proof for your singles, it will make about 2 gal or so this run, repeat the whole process 2 more times or more, don't forget to take some old meal out and put same amount of fresh back in each time and also pour the singles back in the cooker. I don't think I've ever seen the proof get above 140, but have seen 11 gal. yields.

On your very last cooking, pour all your previous runs of the 80-140 in a barrel and run your last cooking, keep adding your makings to the barrel stirring and checking till you get the proof you want, most times we done 97-100 proof. But this could be drinked as is

or if you wanted it much better, you put all of this finished shine back in the cooker and cooked it agin, this time it comes out at 170 proof and let it run to about 150. Take this and put in a barrel and mix well or spring water with it to get the proof down, it still makes about the same amount, 3 runs always made 22-23 gals. REMEMBER NO YEAST WAS ADDED!!!!!!!!!!

....

Rice

A friend of mine wanted me to try and make for him a traditional Korean spirit. I'm not sure how traditional this is, but, judging by the info on ancient Chinese distillation techniques, this stuff would be considered a high quality drink.

Go to an asian food store and look in the fridge section for something called Koji (it's a mold culture used to make soy paste, sake, etc), it typically comes in a plastic, 20oz container (round, taller rather than wider- I used Cold Mountain brand rice koji).

Soak an equal VOLUME of short grain rice in enough water to cover it overnight (just dump the koji into a bowl and use the container to get an equal volume of rice/koji), then, steam the rice for 45minutes. After steaming, add 20fl.oz. of cold water and 1.25teaspoons of Morton Salt Substitute (no other brand is allowed- this is the only stuff with the right chemical composition)

(The salt substitute is a mix of potassium chloride, fumaric acid, tri- and mono- calcium phosphate. It's not essential to the brewing proccess (I've made 2 batches, one with one without- I couldn't tell the difference) as far as I can see, but the book on sake brewing I have reccomends it. If you can't find it- don't worry, for this recipe it's not critical. It's more of a requirement for plain sake brewing, though. I guess it acts like a micronutrient source for the yeast and the koji. The sake book also adds a little winemaker's yeast nutrient, but I ran out while trying out the recipe- it didn't harm it any.)

Stir the rice/water until there are no clumps of grain, then add the koji.

Cover and let it sit for 2 days, then add a wine yeast (I used lalvin k1v-1116).

Allow to ferment at LAGER temperature (50F) until the rice settles down to the bottom of the fermentor.

Distill this sour smelling sake twice in a pot still- that's it- a traditional korean folk liquor. If you use sorghum instead of rice, you get a drink highly prized in China called Mao- Tai. I personally hate sake (I thought tequila hangovers were bad!),but this distilled product is pretty good- It has a buttery, grainy smell/flavor that is really quite good (the sorghum version has the same taste but with an underlying soy flavor- my personal favorite). Forget all the sake you have tried- this stuff has none of the sourness of the mash. It is, in fact, not sweet, but almost malty in texture (like a thick beer-despite being out of a still), and is definitely the strangest batch that you can bring to any homebrew tasting. Something grand from those who brought you Kimchi!!

Well, I hope that you have had fun learning how to make moonshine at home and seeing how it was made in the past, and how it is still being made clandestinely around the world. But be aware that it is an illegal activity in some countries with severe penalties. Japanese rice wine or 'Sake' is distilled to make the spirit 'Shochu' ('Soju' in Korean). Koji mold (Aspergilus ssp.) is traditionally used to make the mash, but enzymes (amylase) and citric acid are also being used currently to make shochu.

....

A Japanese experiment by Kenryo Nishimura and others proved that it is not necessary to cook (to gelatinize) or convert (malting) milled grain prior to fermentation. Milling, soaking, adding enzymes and citric acid is sufficient - "   the product obtained by the

non-cooking fermentation method was superior to that obtained by the cooking fermentation method in terms of both aroma and flavor components." The product referred to is 'shochu', a Japanese distilled spirit from rice. The non-cooking fermentation did take only one day longer than the cooking method due to the initial concentration of glucose in the cooking method. The method eliminates the messy cooking part of using grain and should encourage more to try grain-based washes

....

about Koji ...

Kojiis a type of mould similar to that which turns bread green and furry. Scientific name: Aspergillus oryzae. It breaks down starch with an enzyme called amylase, the same one as in saliva and malted grains (the very same enzymes we activate when we mash malted barley, wheat etc to produce wort.)

Koji comes in two forms. First is koji kin, in other words, seed koji. This is generally in the form of rice grains on which the mould has been allowed to run rampant and go to spore and then dried. This is now the inoculum.

The second form is what is more commonly referred to as simply koji, but to distinguish it from koji kin is referred to as kome koji (kome means rice in Japanese--it is pronounced as two syllables, the "o" should be as in of, and the "e" as in egg.) So this koji is steamed and cooled rice that has been inocculated with some koji kin and then incubated at 30 to 35 degrees for a few days. The mould hyphae grow right through the rice. You need to stir it every 6 to 12 hours and stop it by bunging it in the fridge if it starts to go yellowy green--that means it is trying to form spore. In Japan, it is possible to pop down to the local supermarket and buy koji in this form fromm the cool-goods section as it is used for making miso paste and a few other food-related things.

In sake making, it is this kome koji that is mixed together with a larger quantity of steamed rice, some water and yeast to get the fermentation underway. At coolish temperatures (10-15 deg) the koji chugs away making amylase, the amylase converts the rice starch to sugar, and the yeast does what yeast does best.

....

Bread (From 'waste' products)

Wal writes ...

Bread is already a baked (cooked) milled grain i.e flour, and seems like an great waste product to ferment. At least 50% starch apparently.

I collected over a period 7kg of left-over bread. Dried it to make sure it did not go mouldy, and just treated it like a milled and cooked grain. You have the option of adding 10% malt to convert the starch to sugars or using amylase enzymes. Yield is apparently about 60% sugar from the starch in the bread. I used 1 kg bread/5 litres of water. (1 lb - 2 lb/gal seems the norm)

Method:

Crush bread (gelatines easier)

Raise temperature of water to 75C (I used a 60 liter HDPE open-top plastic drum with 2/1500W jug elements screwed in)

Add crushed bread

Wait for temperature to drop to 65C

Add malt or amylase enzymes (I used enzymes) Hold at 65C for at least 1 hour.

Cool to 24C (overnight)

Add yeast (You could first strain off the sugar rich liquid for a clean wash)

Left over bread can also be used as a supplement with a sugar wash to provide nutrients for the yeast.

....

Bouza (Egyptian beer):

To get a 5% abv beer you would use 4 kg coarsely ground wheat

1 kg wheat grain 30 liters water

Knead 4 kg coarse flour with a quantiity of water into a dough. Cut dough into thick loaves and bake lightly.

Moisten with water the 1 kg of wheat grain and allow to germinate (3-5 days).

Sun dry grains, crush and mix with the bread loaves which are soaked in water in a fermenter.

Add active slurry from previous mash. Ferment. Bread is also still fermented to make a 'bread kvas' by the Eastern Slavs (Ukrainians, Belarusians, Russians) and the word 'kvas' is mentioned in 10th century Kievan chronicles. 'Kvas' is a generic word covering weakly fermented drinks from malted grain, bread, fruits and tree saps (maple & birch). Red beets were also fermented to make a sour 'beet kvas' for borshch before the introduction of tomatoes which provided sourness. 'Bread kvas' which is allowed to go sour, is also used as a natural vinegar for borshch. Sometimes one comes across the word 'kvas' and for comparison purposes here are several redacted recipes.

....

Green malt and rye bread kvas:

1 kg green rye malt (barley & oats were also malted) 1 kg sliced dried dark rye bread

20 liters water

For a reddish color, roast a small quantity of the malted grain) Crush malt lightly. Add green malt and bread to water (65C). Allow to stand for several hours. Add sour dough starter (or 30 g yeast) and allow to ferment for several days. Strain. Keep in cool place. Drink when still effervescent or bottle as for beer.

.... Rye bread kvas:

1 kg sliced dried rye bread (lightly toasted in oven) 1 kg honey, molasses (or sugar)

20 litres water

Pour boiling water over bread, honey/molasses. Allow to cool (24C). Add sour dough starter (or 30 g yeast) and allow to ferment for several days. Strain. Keep in cool place.

....

Crabapple and wild pear kvas:

7.5 kg apples (cores removed)

7.5 kg pears (cores removed) 20 litres water

Pour water over apples and pears. Cover and allow to ferment (traditionally by wild yeasts). Strain. Keep in cool place. Drink when still effervescent or bottle as for beer.

Kvas is a folk beverage, and there are many variations depending on available material and personal taste. I have seen recipes using mint or horseradish root for flavoring.

....

WHEAT GERM RECIPE

1 jar 20oz. of wheat germ this can be found by the oatmeal in most grocery stores

2oz. of an acid blend witch has citric acid, malic acid and another this can be found in any liqour stores that sell home brewing stuff

5 lbs sugar the cheep stuff works just as good as the name brand and 5 gallons of water

1oz of bear yeast

All you need to do is steep in water at 180 degrees all of the ingredients except for the yeast for about 30 min while that is steeping put the packet of yeast in a glass of room temperature water as instructed on the packet of yeast after the mix cools filter it into a 6 1/2 gallon glass jar to remove the wheat germ and add the yeast the mix must be no hotter than 80 degrees F and no cooler than 65 F degrees or the yeast will die. Check the yeast package for proper temperature. Place a bubbler in the top of the jar when it stops bubbling the mix is ready to distill or is a very good wine that taste like pears. This is the easiest recipe I have found. It's a moon-shiners dream.

....END OF FRUIT & GRAIN
....

OTHER REFRENCES

References:

The differences between Scotch whisky, Irish and American whiskeys is outlined at 'The Macallan' site:http://www.themacallan-themalt.com/.

See also ...

Avoiding Post-Fermentation Problems How the Mash Makes Wort

Boiling and Hops Bodensatz Brewing

Ian Smiley "Making Pure Corn Whisky" (http://www.home-distilling.com/)